CW01096088

MARLOW
PAST & PRESENT

BARBARA RICHARDSON
& CECELIA ANNE SADEK

The History Press

Time present and time past
Are both perhaps present in time future,
And time future contained in time past.
T.S. Eliot

This memorial stone, erected in the
churchyard of All Saints' in 1995,
commemorates poet T.S. Eliot, who
lived in Marlow in 1916 at the Old
Post Office House, 31 West Street. The
excerpt engraved on the stone in the
photograph is taken from his poem
'Burnt Norton' from the *Four Quartets*.
The *Four Quartets* were published over
a six-year period, three being written
during Second World War air raids.

To our families and friends for their love and support

First published 2010

The History Press
The Mill, Brimscombe Port
Stroud, Gloucestershire, GL5 2QG
www.thehistorypress.co.uk

British Library Cataloguing in Publication Data.
A catalogue record for this book is available from the British Library.

ISBN 978 0 7524 5284 5

Typesetting and origination by The History Press
Printed in Great Britain
Manufacturing managed by Jellyfish Print Solutions Ltd

CONTENTS

ACKNOWLEDGEMENTS

For their help with the research, historical study and archive work by the authors, thanks are given to Buckinghamshire County Council for supplying the old photographs; to the Buckinghamshire County Librarian's team for their help and advice; the Marlow Society; High Wycombe Local Studies; *Bucks Free Press*; English Heritage; the National Monument Records; and the Francis Frith Collection for supply of old photographs and copyright permission. Thanks are given for the lending of old and new photographs, copyright permissions, historical and current information to: Horsham Museum; Peter and Billy Pinches; June Coleridge; Mrs Wendy Ball; Jim Platt; Bernard Burger; Rachel Browne: John Laker; John Colverson; Brian Drage; Peter McArdle; Tony Buzan; Sir Steve Redgrave; Heston Blumenthal; Peter Jones; and the Rebellion Beer Co. For taking some of the new photographs and copyright permission, our sincere thanks go to Vincent Alexander Mitchell. Finally and most importantly, many thanks to our publishers for their forbearance while we struggled to give this project its deserved priority in our ridiculously busy lives.

ABOUT THE AUTHORS

Cecelia Anne Sadek grew up at Quarry Dale in Marlow. She is a published poet and founder of the Marlow Poetry Society. She has regularly organised and taken part in art, charity and poetry events and continues to follow her passion as a writer and musician. Cecelia headed the Marlow Poets' contribution of written and spoken poetry for a local Millennium Exhibition presented and archived for the century ahead. She is currently working on a new collection of adult and children's books of poetry. As a friend of Marlow FM radio, she plans to present a regular literature and poetry show. Cecelia runs Serendipity Sales Solutions, offering sales and marketing along with web design services to local and international businesses. Her love for Marlow's beautiful countryside and local community inspired her to write this book.

When Barbara Richardson moved to Marlow in 1990, she was quickly provided with the excellent book *A Pictorial History of Marlow* by Julian Hunt and Rachel Browne. Walking around her new home town, she was continually struck by the degree to which Marlow's buildings had not fundamentally changed since the times portrayed in the old photos and pictures in that book. She began to think how good it would be to compile a book showing the modern equivalents of the old views and link the two views with a couple of paragraphs. As a chartered surveyor, she is particularly interested in town development, having worked as a Development Director in London's West End in the 1980s for Sibec Developments, creators of shopping centres and town centre redevelopments. As Thames Property Solutions Ltd, she promoted a comprehensive redevelopment of the site including and around the Waitrose store on West Street before Sainsbury got involved.

She now runs three websites: www.downsizeproperty.co.uk, www.alchemy.me.uk and www.advantagebusinessnetworking.co.uk. She has published articles and short stories before and, following this most recent experience, even her poetry may now see the light of day.

INTRODUCTION

Marlow as a twenty-first-century town might, at first glance, appear to be almost as unrecognisable from its nineteenth- and twentieth-century selves, as 'Marlow' is from its original name of 'Mewrelafam', a Saxon word meaning 'land of the lakes'. Archaeological evidence does not stretch to providing the name given to the area by Marlow's first inhabitants, who arrived 10,000 years ago, but you can be sure that they would be bemused by the sheer number of people living here today (around 20,000) as well as by the retail, leisure, information technology and other commercial activities which have taken over from agriculture.

The river as a giver of life started the story, followed swiftly by the river as a highway, boundary, provider of food, power source and a means to earn a living. The earliest known industries were lace-making, water extraction, paper milling and brewing. Marlow's progression through the years has also been driven by its powerful and influential residents and their contacts with the Royal Court at Windsor. Agriculture gave way to commerce and industry, which in turn have ceded space to homes, with both new and existing residential areas seeing the density of development increase significantly in the late twentieth century.

Alongside these physical changes, there have been major social changes. Marlow has witnessed the exodus from London, the increase in commuting back into the City and the changing profile of women in the family and in the community. Marlow has always had its share of famous people and this has continued in recent years, with twenty-first-century celebrity taking its place alongside academics, poets and extraordinary athletic achievement.

Extensive commercial operations, quality retailing, excellent hotels and accommodation, and incredible opportunities for eating and drinking, crossing most cultures, all make for a Marlow that is considerably more sophisticated than its prosaic beginnings. At its heart though, Marlow is still all about the river. Its life and movement, its associated wildlife, its changing seasons and its accessibility make Marlow an attractive place to live, work and spend time. A closer look at Marlow reveals how the essence of this riverside town has remained intact and, over the centuries, has evolved from its past to its present-day 'Marlovian' self.

William the Conqueror's Domesday Book relates the value of Marlow as £25. An estimate today would run into many millions. How Marlow has changed, and how Marlow has stayed the same...

1

GEOGRAPHY

A view of the River Thames at Marlow, looking south-east from the tower of All Saints' Church. The aerial view shows both banks of the River Thames and the weir with Winter Hill and Bisham Woods surrounding the fields beyond, on the outskirts of Marlow. Marlow Lock is hidden behind the trees, but the wooden footbridge to reach Lock Island and the apartment complex which replaced Marlow Mill can clearly be seen, as can the river east of the lock. The river gives its name to the Thames Valley, a region of England centred around the river between Oxford and West London, and the Thames Estuary, to the east of London. This aerial photograph was taken around 1970.

The Romans invaded Britain in AD 43 and left behind weapons, tools and pottery which have since been recovered from the river at Marlow, along with those of their predecessors, the Saxons. The Thames in those days was an established method of transport, not least because the local topography allowed for the building of a flash lock (a method of navigating water by opening part of the weir), part of which is still visible today. The weir was designed to hold back water for the mill and the lock was highly dangerous for navigation, involving as it did a sharp turn under the bridge. Many accidents, some fatal, have been recorded. In 1700 the weir was replaced by earth and timber locks. All Saints' Church stands tall in the background and to its left the suspension bridge links the two counties of Buckinghamshire and Berkshire.

The weir today is approximately on the same site and continues to play an important role in controlling the flow of water and helping to prevent flooding. Today the river is used purely for leisure and you can stroll beside the water, watching the boats and cruising barges travel up and down. At the weekends and on Bank Holidays, the river is as busy with these craft as it can ever have been with the commercial craft of the past.

Above left: This photograph shows the river frontage of St Peter Street, formerly known as Duck Lane, which was the site of the old wooden bridge across the River Thames before the suspension bridge was built. This photograph was taken in 1870.

Above right: This original hand-coloured print dates back to between 1800 and 1809 and shows a stylised view of the old wooden bridge from St Peter Street and the parish church beyond. In the foreground a man is poling a punt across the River Thames in front of the single weir. Eel bucks are attached to the bridge for catching eels. According to the Domesday Survey, the manor of Marlow enjoyed the profits from 1,000 eels per year, probably caught in eel bucks similar to the ones shown in the picture.

St Peter Street is one of the oldest streets in Marlow and the original and subsequent bridges sprang from its southern end across the river. It was also called Bridge Street in the 1700s. On the river bank stood a large winch which was used for hauling barges upstream through the flash lock. The old cottages would accommodate bargemen, brewers' labourers and workers at the mills. Many floods have been witnessed in this street due to the Thames overflowing as it rose above the street level. Looking south-east, this photograph, taken in 1900, shows a crowd of residents and local people near the Two Brewers public house during such a flooding. A wooden contraption has been used to help residents cross the street.

St Peter Street in 2010 with the Two Brewers pub, currently run by Anthony Burnham. Since 1755, the Two Brewers has been refreshing the thirsty and the downright sociable on the side of the River Thames in Marlow. Over 255 years on, this tradition is still maintained at the Two Brewers. Today, the English gastropub serves food and stocks a range of real ales, plus lagers and ciders by well-known UK based breweries alongside international brands. Flooding still occurs on this street.

Marlow High Street on a busy day, looking north up from the river and the suspension bridge towards the top of the street, where the Crown Hotel can be seen in the centre of the photograph in 1905. Many interesting old houses line the street dating back from the sixteenth, seventeenth and eighteenth centuries. In the early nineteenth century, a stage-coach called 'The Marlow Flier' operated a twice-daily service to London from High Street. The journey from Marlow to Piccadilly took around three hours. Although heavy goods were still carried more efficiently by water, road transport became the best means of carrying goods and people rapidly and safely between the booming towns of late eighteenth- and early nineteenth-century England. In the early twentieth century, the population of Great Marlow was recorded at 5,645 people.

The heart of the town and the central shopping area is as lively today as it was 105 years ago. The basic geography of Marlow has not changed in this part of town. Over the years alterations have been made to some buildings and their shop fronts. The wide pavements and general appearance of the High Street is very similar to how it was in 1905, except for the dominance of the motor car.

High Street looking south towards the river in 1920, showing shoppers on both sides of the street and a man on his tricycle. The view of the High Street as far as the Causeway includes Sayer Bros, who were provision merchants, and W.R. Clark, a butcher's shop, at No. 22 and No. 24. Because of the limited number of motor vehicles on the roads in those days, it was common for people and shoppers to walk casually on the roads as well as the pavements. This photograph appears to have been taken from an elevated position.

High Street looking south in 2010 looks remarkably similar to ninety years ago when, at the time, England was recovering from the shock and devastation of the First World War. Since then local butchers, fishmongers, grocers and many other provisional shops have all died out and been replaced by the modern shops, supermarkets, boutiques and restaurants that we typically see today. Marlow High Street is one of approximately 5,500 High Streets in the UK. The name High Street tops the street-name charts, being the most common street name across Britain.

Quoiting Square, Marlow.

Quoiting Square stands at the junction of West Street and Oxford Road, making what used to be a pleasant open space in the middle of the town. The square itself may have been used to play quoits, which is a traditional lawn game involving the throwing of a metal or rubber ring over a set distance to land over a pin in the centre of a patch of clay. There is evidence that a similar game was played by Ancient Greeks and Romans before it spread to Britain.

The house that gave its name to Quoiting Square was redeveloped in the early Noughties into flats. The attractive double-fronted house shown in the old photograph facing down the Square has been demolished and some of the buildings have been replaced, although the west-facing elevation looks remarkably recognisable. Platts' forecourt is shown on the left, where new and used cars are for sale and petrol supplies are available (and have been since 1920). The old pumps were hand cranked before the introduction of the electric-powered fuel pumps we use today. The petrol forecourt is one of the very few in the country to remain operator served.

West Street looking east in 1900. Its old gas lamp on the left-hand corner of Oxford Road would be lit every evening. Before electricity became sufficiently widespread and economical to allow for general public use, gas was the most popular means of lighting in cities and suburbs. Early gas lights had to be lit manually but soon they could light themselves.

Over a century later, high-standard lamps are commonly in use and rise to the top of the buildings, along with the latest Closed Circuit Television cameras (CCTV) installed in the centre of town to keep a watchful eye. The old Queen drinking house is now a residential property. West Street is a great mix of shops, residential and commercial properties and businesses.

West Street becomes Henley Road at its residential end and leads out of Marlow to Henley-on-Thames, c. 1896. Beautiful old cottages and listed buildings are found along this street. The stage-coach would have regularly travelled back and forth this way on its journey between Henley and London.

Comparing both photographs, this one taken in 2009 reveals a very similar scene albeit with the addition of traffic signals for safe pedestrian crossing to the local Grammar School. West Street still provides the principal scenic route in and out of the town. The historic Albion House (front right) takes its name from Albion (a Greek word) which was the oldest known name of the island of Great Britain. It is sometimes used poetically today to refer to England, appropriately linking its literary connections with the house and its past occupants.

In 1910 this photograph shows the eastern end of West Street towards its junction with High Street and Spittal Street. Horse-drawn carts and a horse and rider can be seen making their leisurely way along the road. Overall, Marlow's architecture does not seem to have altered.

Today, mostly retail outlets line this end of West Street and include Waitrose supermarket on the left-hand side, with various boutiques, local pubs and shops opposite. The clock tower at the top of the old Crown Hotel is clearly visible protruding above the rest of the buildings.

Spittal Street looking east shows a scene of shoppers, cyclists and a cart in 1912. In those days children could stand fairly safely on the road unperturbed by traffic, unlike the younger generation of today.

Spittal Street is still a busy shopping street with the same narrow pavements, but with much heavier traffic. It is one of three main routes in and out of Marlow. Small alleyways dart off in various parts to lead into the back streets and other areas of the town.

Chapel Street, looking east in 1900, was probably named after the Chantry Chapel, known to have been founded in the medieval period. There was a tollhouse in Chapel Street and in 1826 it is recorded that the toll was 4*d* for a horse and carriage, cattle were 10*d* a score, and sheep and pigs were 5*d* a score. Mail coaches, parish traffic and clergymen all passed free. Many tollhouses were built by turnpike trusts in England during the eighteenth and early nineteenth centuries. In 1840, the Turnpike Returns in Parliamentary Papers recorded 5,000 tollhouses operating in England. These were sold off in the 1880s when the turnpikes were closed.

Chapel Street in 2010 is a busy main road leading in and out of Marlow. It is still principally residential with terraced houses dating back to Victorian times, along with commercial offices and several shops on its south side. Visitors can be seen waiting at the bus stop, one of several stops en route to and from the town centre.

Dean Street in 1917 looking north-west shows the Mint public house, which supplied Wethered's Marlow ales, opposite a small grocery supplier and mostly residential properties. Dean Street, along with Chapel Street, provided housing to the poor and these were known as the poor houses where the majority of Marlow's community would have lived. In 1608, it is known that John Brinkhurst founded almshouses for the poor in Marlow. There were several other benefactions belonging to the town, one of which included money left by Mr Loftin in 1759 for the purpose of apprenticing poor children. The Poor Law Amendment Act of 1834 was brought in for the relief of the poor and derived from previous Elizabethan laws.

Dean Street in 2010 appears to be barely recognisable, with its car park on the right-hand side in place of the old cottages. The buildings at the front left-hand side are the only evidence remaining of the original Dean Street.

2

TRADE AND INDUSTRY

Thomas Wethered seated in a chair in his studio in 1802. Thomas Wethered & Sons, established in 1758, represented the important brewing industry in Marlow. Its heritage dates back over 250 years. According to the returns made to Parliament under the Population Act in 1801, the town and parish of Great Marlow contained 643 houses, of which twenty-six were uninhabited. The number of inhabitants was 3,236, of whom 1,436 were males and 1,800 females. The number of persons employed chiefly in agriculture was 236, with 306 in trade, manufacture, and handicraft.

Malt was grown in Marlow and shipped down the Thames to London brewers. Eventually local maltsters started breweries in Marlow, of which the principal brewery came to be Wethereds, set up by George Wethered around the middle of the 1700s. It became Thomas Wethered & Sons in 1758, and produced 25,000 barrels of beer a year. Thomas died in 1849, leaving a fortune of £100,000, equivalent to £77 million today. The brewery passed to Owen Wethered in 1851. The building shown in this photograph taken in 1940 was the headquarters of the brewery, which finally closed in 1988.

The main brewery building has in the past twenty-two years housed offices, with a number of businesses occupying the three floors. The building on the left, known as the Old Brewery offices, is now Zizzi's restaurant, which has retained the original high ceilings and has a large, open kitchen with a clay oven.

Above left: The storeroom at Wethered Brewery in 1850 shows Wethered's racking or cask-filling room under the brewery building. This became a car park for the residents of the redeveloped brewery when it was converted to residential use.

Above right: The tradition of brewing in Marlow looked like coming to an end after the closure of Wethereds in 1988 until two local men, Tim Coombes and Mark Gloyens, developed a plan for a new Marlow brewery to be called the Rebellion Beer Co. In 1993 it opened on the Rose Business Estate in Marlow Bottom, surrounded by the chalky Chiltern Hills which provide water high in minerals and salts, essential for producing high quality and distinctive real ale. The brewery expanded and moved to long-term premises at Bencombe Farm. This photograph shows the racking room in 2009. Brewing on average reaches 175 barrels of beer per week, and is sold locally to over 200 pubs within a thirty-mile radius of Marlow and through the brewery shop.

Above left: Wethered Brewery staff standing outside the brewery tower in the 1850s.

Above right: Staff and family members of the Rebellion Beer Co. in 2003. One of the owners, Tim Coombes, is third from left in the back row.

In the early eighteenth century, three mills dominated Marlow's industry: a corn mill, an oil mill processing flax and rape seed and a brass thimble mill owned by Dutchman John Lofting. The river delivered raw materials to Marlow as well as finished goods to London. The oil and thimble mills were eventually replaced by paper mills, the last of which closed in 1965. Thomas Williams, the copper baron, manufactured brass and copper pans and thimbles at Temple Mills, near Marlow, using copper extracted from his mines in Anglesey. This photograph taken in the early 1900s shows a view across the millpond to the corn and paper mills.

Modern houses named 'Marlow Mills' were built on the same site as the old mills alongside Marlow Lock.

This photograph taken in 1855 shows Queen Victoria and her eldest daughter, Princess Vicky, whose trousseau contained lace made in Marlow, for which it was famous. Black lace was famously first created in Marlow. Lace-making was primarily an industry of women home-workers. Regular visits from the lace collector with his packhorse, bringing stocks of raw materials and money with which to pay the lace-makers, was to be a feature of local life for three centuries. Note the huge circumference of their crinoline-supported skirts!

Street frontage of the premises of Webb's the corn merchant at 11 Dean Street, photographed in 1910. The corn mills on the river would have supplied its produce to Webb's for local consumption.

Venture Portraits in 2009, supplying family portrait photography. It was opened in 1999 at 11 Dean Street by owners Michelle O'Sullivan and Elaine Mulvaney.

The premises of Warner & Drye carriage builders and wheelwrights at 19 High Street in 1890, with their new four-wheeled carriage outside. Some ten years later, they started to repair motor cars.

No. 19 High Street is today the home of WHSmith, which was the first chain store company in the world and was responsible for the creation of the ISBN book catalogue system.

Above left: In 1895 the 'Three Lions' were named after the closely positioned pubs on West Street: the Red Lion on the left, opposite the White Lion and Black Lion (front right), which was to become R.J.E. Platt in 1925. It initially sold Bush, Murphy and Pye radio equipment and later motor cars and petrol, as it continues to do so today.

Above right: This recent photograph shows Platts motor car sales and service business, which was developed during the 1920s and 1930s. In 1985 Platts were approached by Ford Motor Co. to become main dealers for the area. Since then the used car sales area and showroom have been expanded. Servicing and repairs moved to their Oxford Road premises, which were extended in the 1960s.

This photograph shows Mrs Audrey Platt, wife of Jim Platt, who is at the front beside his father, Reginald James Edward Platt, founder of R.J.E. Platt, after their return from a British Leyland car rally to Belgium in 1975. During the Second World War, as well as running the garage and wartime production of electric motors, Reg was a member of the auxiliary Thames River Patrol, based at Marlow Rowing Club. Bevan James Platt (known as Jim Platt) joined Platts of Marlow in 1959. For many years Jim was mainly involved with the Service Department before taking overall control of the business when his father retired in 1983. Jim rowed for Marlow Rowing Club and was an active member of Marlow Rugby Club, in charge of fundraising. Platts itself is one of only a few long-established, family-run businesses left in Marlow today.

After the Reformation, Widmere Farm belonged for some time to the Widmeres, an ancient family who seem to have taken their name from the place. The twelfth-century chapel with its crypt still remains attached to the farmhouse and is considered to be the oldest surviving structure in the parish of Marlow. Sir William Borlase, who was Lord of the Manor of Marlow at the time, bought Widmere in 1623. Subsequently John Borlase, MP for Marlow, held a court at Widmere in 1671. The farm passed to the Temples of Stowe and was purchased in 1766 by William Clayton. Having originally been a mixed farm, it is now arable. This change has been driven by economics, with many farms in the area following the same path. In addition, farmland is now often being used as paddocks for horses owned for recreational purposes.

The crypt shown in this recent photograph is accessed down a flight of wooden stairs, which arrives at a series of columns, pillars and archways. The two recesses at the western end may have been used to house the caskets and coffins of important people. The crypt experienced many uses, including being a dairy in relatively recent times. The upper floor of the crypt was discovered to have been a ceiling hiding the extensive network of medieval beams and timberwork. Worn remnants, and a pristine tile found nearby, indicate they date from the mid-fourteenth century. It is thought that the Knights Templar may have built the chapel, or that it was possibly a Saxon chapel further modified in Norman times.

Tommy Morris reared animals on his local farm, Barmoor, on the outskirts of Marlow. He owned and ran three butcher's shops in Marlow, including T. Morris in Spittal Street, for twenty-six years, as shown in this 1920 photograph. Tommy is fourth from the right. His wife, first on the left, and two sons, Stanley and Baden, are shown fourth and sixth from the left respectively alongside other members of staff.

Tommy Morris' Prize Bull won a competition in the 1919 local fat stock show, an annual event in the area. This photograph was taken at the back of Liston Court, opposite Morris' butcher's shop. The manager, David White, stands proudly beside members of staff.

Francesco's Italian restaurant at 13 Spittal Street has been here for more than twenty years. Franco Anitinoro, the owner, was born in Sicily and came to England in 1968 with the intention of bringing the taste of the Mediterranean to the English palate. He has two more restaurants in nearby Maidenhead and Windsor.

Above: This photograph taken in 1935 shows Fieldhouse Farm in Fieldhouse Lane. It was established in 1919 as a dairy farm by Billy Pinches, a horse dealer. It also became the Marlow Riding School in 1932. Billy was known to ask the local stationmaster to hold the train if he was running late as Fieldhouse Farm was one of the railway's biggest customers. A considerable amount of business was done with them, with horses from as far as Shropshire being brought down in special horse boxes. In those days, very few residents had a telephone and the local police station would dial 63 through the local exchange to Billy in order to get messages relayed to the local bobby on his beat nearby.

Left: Peter Pinches, son of Billy, in 1928 at the farm with his pet monkey, Jenny. She was a very friendly animal with male company but she notoriously disliked any females in the household. Their eccentric neighbour was known to keep a giraffe and other exotic animals.

In 1970 Raymond Mold from Arlington Securities, an investment and development company, approached Mr Pinches with a proposal to develop the first out-of-town business park in the country. The Pinches' farm was key to the whole development because they owned the land. Following a long-drawn-out but eventually successful planning process, the land was sold to Arlington Securities which named the development Globe Park in 1975.

Globe Park created an explosion in Marlow itself. It changed progressively from a sleepy riverside market town to a popular commuter and industrial town where people wanted to work and live. The population has trebled since then. Thames Industrial Estate and Globe Business Park play host to a mixture of manufacturing, service and professional organisations. For example, Peter Jones of *Dragon's Den* fame has his Phones International business here, as shown in the photograph taken in 2009.

Peter Jones, a Marlow entrepreneur, lives in Marlow with his partner and three daughters. He says he is most proud of his family and his biggest success has been bringing his beautiful kids into this world: 'It truly beats anything that I've ever done in business.' He likes to spend time with his family and says he loves Marlow town centre, often walking in the park and down by the river with his family. He considers Marlow to be one of the most beautiful towns in the country.

Above left: Miss Graft, a local authoress, seated on Midnight, a horse belonging to the Marlow Riding School. Sadly, Midnight was put down following a broken leg not long after this photograph was taken in 1936 at Fieldhouse Farm, where the new Globe Park Development was to be built some forty years later. No. 3 Quarry Dale Drive can be seen on the left-hand side. It was one of several houses overlooking the farm.

Above right: Milk supplies from Fieldhouse Farm were delivered daily to local residents. Here, young Benny West is sitting on the 'New Milk' cart in 1920. He would accompany the local milkman on his rounds.

Globe Park in 2010, photographed from the same position as above left. This broad area of Marlow, redeveloped for business use, has radically altered the land beyond recognition.

3

TRANSPORT

West Street, with a view of a liveried horse and carriage outside the Red Lion Hotel, *c.* 1928. The era of the stage-coach covered the 200 years between the restoration of the monarchy and the coming of the railways. A stage-coach in the late seventeenth century would take nearly two days to reach London. Creating a network of well-maintained roads was one of the major achievements of eighteenth-century England and included a comprehensive network of turnpike roads built across Britain. These linked the major centres of population by highways which facilitated the rapid and efficient transportation of goods and passengers throughout the kingdom. This facilitated the transition between the river and road transport. Bodies of local trustees were given powers to levy tolls on the users of a specified stretch of road to improve and maintain that particular section of the turnpike network.

The Great Western Railway transformed the coaching trade consisting of stage-coaches and carrier carts travelling between Marlow and Maidenhead. The railway finally reached Marlow around 1872 with the arrival of the 'Marlow Donkey', the nickname given to the steam locomotive. Privately funded, the Great Marlow Railway Co. was established to provide a transport link to join Maidenhead to the High Wycombe branch of the GWR at Bourne End (no longer in existence). For over a century, the steam train would be laden with people, goods and coal. In the 1970s, it would be replaced by self-contained diesel engine carriages, carrying only people. The railway, providing a commuter route to London, encouraged the influx of wealthy families to Marlow.

Above left: The original station was built but then demolished in 1968 to help facilitate the development of the industrial estate. An office block has been built on the foundations of the station buildings, now containing the Pink Accountancy Co. The railway branch still remains without the station.

Above right: The Marlow branch line is a commuter route for many Marlow residents travelling to London and the City via Bourne End and Maidenhead, thus securing the position of Marlow as an attractive commuter town.

Staff of the Great Marlow Railway at the railway station, Great Marlow, *c.* 1892.

The 'Marlow Donkey' at Marlow Station in Station Road, *c.* 1910. Railway workers and passengers look towards the camera in this romantic setting with old lamps, benches and milk churns gracing the platform on this side of the railway track.

RAILWAY HOTEL, MARLOW-ON-THAMES.

Looking south on Station Road, a view of the Railway Hotel with several four-wheeled horse-drawn carriages, *c.* 1900. The Railway Hotel was later named the Marlow Donkey.

A view of the Marlow Donkey pub at the junction of Glade Road and Station Road, photographed in 2010. This popular pub is close to the station and has a good range of food and a large garden.

Above left: The current Marlow bridge is a suspension bridge and was designed and supervised during construction by William Tierney Clark in 1832 to replace the old wooden bridge sited further downstream, which had grown inadequate for the increasing traffic on the Reading and Hatfield Turnpike Road. It was demolished in 1828. The new iron bridge was a prototype for the nearly identical but larger Széchenyi Chain Bridge across the River Danube in Budapest. In the 1950s it was proposed to replace the Suspension Bridge with a ferro-concrete span, and the Marlow Bridge Preservation Committee (from which The Marlow Society arose) was formed to oppose this plan. In 1965 the Suspension Bridge was faithfully reconstructed by Buckinghamshire County Council. A typical journey across Marlow's suspension bridge is shown in this photograph, taken during repairs which had followed a succession of unsafe declarations.

Above right: Marlow Bridge today continues to be a scenic route across the River Thames. There are walkways either side for people to cross on foot and to view the river, boating activity and local wildlife. At New Year the bridge is closed for fifteen minutes due to the number of people standing on the bridge to see the firework display.

Above left: This photograph, taken around 1932, shows a typical horse and cart at the bottom of the yard at Fieldhouse Farm.

Above right: Modern agricultural farm equipment and machinery used throughout England today includes this Massey Ferguson farm tractor. The company was responsible for producing the world's first commercially successful self-propelled combine in 1938.

Above left: Peter Pinches' dung cart at Fieldhouse Farm, used for transporting manure in the stables. On this occasion, without any other transport available, it was used to collect guests who had arrived at Marlow Railway Station. This photograph was taken around 1935 and shows the passengers not in the slightest bit put out and quite enjoying the ride.

Above right: Taken in 2010 outside the Thai Square restaurant, formerly the Red Lion Hotel, this photograph shows the luxury way of transporting passengers today in a modern-day taxi on a typical late evening. M.K. Marlow Taxis, established in 1998 and run by Ghalib Hussain, provides services to both local residents and businesses.

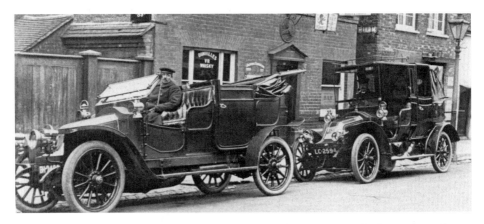

The Ford Motor Co. had an engine running by 1893, and the first car was built in 1896 and went into production for sale to the public in 1903. During the post-war era, cars like the Morris Minor soon became popular throughout the UK. In 1913 the first Morris car was produced at Cowley in Oxford and 450 cars were made that year. Ten years later production had risen to 20,000. This photograph shows two motor cars (cabs), with their drivers, outside the Red Lion Hotel in West Street, *c.* 1910. The pre-1914 motor cars replaced the Red Lion carriage.

In 2001, the 5,125 households in south and south-east area of Marlow were recorded as owning 7,241 cars and vans between them. Add this to the number of vehicles travelling through Marlow and one can appreciate the extent to which congestion is a major problem. This local resident, who is travelling on the pavement of the High Street on her motorised scooter early one quiet morning, looks to have sensibly chosen the right time to avoid the crowded streets.

4

HOUSES AND HOUSING

All references to The Old Parsonage describe it as possibly the finest medieval survival in Buckinghamshire, dating from the fourteenth century. This is a view looking south across the rear garden, probably taken in the 1920s. It is currently occupied by Mrs Capaldi, widow of Jim Capaldi (2 August 1944-28 January 2005). He was an English musician and songwriter (of Italian parents) and a founding member of Traffic. He drummed with Jimi Hendrix, Eric Clapton and George Harrison amongst others. His solo single, a cover version of The Everly Brothers' 'Love Hurts', rose to number five in the UK charts in October 1975. He was known for his strong lyrics on the subjects of the environment, government corruption and drugs.

In 1900, a Victorian leisure user of Marlow Lock makes his way in a small rowing boat past the Marlow lockkeeper's cottage, watched only by a chap reading a newspaper.

On a hot summer's day in July 2005, a cabin cruiser and a narrow boat make the same journey, closely supervised by the lockkeeper. The lock is used continuously throughout the summer by the large number of small boats owned by people looking for the relative peace and quiet of the river. The fascination of watching the boat owners use a system designed in the eighteenth century attracts many people to simply idle away their time on the side of the lock. Some bring picnics, some still bring the newspaper, but all seem to appreciate the relatively slower pace of life which the lock represents.

The two rather grand Victorian houses with blinds to keep out the south-westerly sun shown in the old photograph, The Sycamores and The Garth on Mill Road, have fallen prey to the intensification of use found across Marlow since this photograph was taken.

In 1965 The Sycamores was converted to two flats, with the original lady occupier eventually living in the ground-floor flat. In that same year of abundant planning permissions for increasing use, permission was granted to build two houses, associated garages and four lock-up garages on land to the rear of The Garth.

In 1998, this was a statutory Conservation Area and Betty Ennis lived in Flat 2, The Sycamores. In 1999, the Revd M. Northwood was living at The Garth, which had by then been listed by English Heritage as being of architectural or historical merit. Sir Keith and Lady Stuart were living in Weir Cottage next door, similarly listed by this time.

Residential development in St Peter Street started with the first planning permission granted in St Peter Street under the 1947 Town and Country Planning Act, allowing the addition of a water closet at the rear of The Minnows.

Despite this small and inauspicious start (unless, of course, you lived at The Minnows), the eye of the development storm settled on St Peter Street between 1964 and 1967. During this period, permission was granted for eighteen flats and seventy-one houses. Wholesale and intensive redevelopment was the order of the day, although the change of use for one house to a country club was refused in 1968.

Throughout this development and increasing numbers of homes, St Peter Street has largely retained its integrity and its dignity. The Two Brewers pub in 2010 looks much as it did in 1832.

The Minnows sold in 2007 for £1.1 million, presumably with the water closet now slightly improved.

Thames Lawn was built in 1770 as a fine three-storey house but the top storey was removed around 1800. A conquering admiral from the Battle of Trafalgar purchased it in 1811 with his prize money.

Above left: It was owned from 1945 by property developer Jack Cotton until his death in 1964. He will have observed the frenzy of development in St Peter Street in the 1960s, when this photograph was taken, but his application to develop up to ten houses in the grounds was turned down.

In 1990, an attempt was made to convert the swimming pool into a private motor museum. The house was bought by Japanese developers for refurbishment early in the 1990s and sold by them to Bushbuy in 1992. In 1995, after three years of hard work with the Conservation Officer and English Heritage, Bushbuy secured planning permission to rebuild Thames Lawn, returned to its original three storeys.

Dr and Mrs David Gabbay bought the Thames Lawn site shortly afterwards. Despite the extent of planning work to replicate the original house, they went on to secure planning permission for the modern mansion shown in the picture.

Above right: A photograph from 1992 of the fire at Thames Bank House, later known as Thames Lawn, with flames coming through the roof. It preceded the sale to Bushbuy Ltd, Marlow-based developers.

The End House at 102 High Street is a Grade II-listed Georgian period town house, built in the eighteenth century, and it stands at the entrance to High Street from the river. It was listed on 16 July 1949.

Above left: It is distinguished by its very lack of change over the fifty years between these two photographs. It is still occupied as a family home and is on the market for £1,595,000 at the time of writing.

Above right: A plaque on Brampton House, next door at 100 High Street, commemorates one famous resident, Edward John Gregory, the internationally-acclaimed artist. He is most famous for his oil painting 'Boulters Lock – Sunday Afternoon', which took seven years to finish. He was also a skilled watercolour artist and became the President of the Royal Institute of Painters in Watercolours in 1898. He died in Brampton House in 1909. He was buried at All Saints' Church by the river.

The change in ownership of Western House, West Street, from a gentleman farmer and his family in 1850 to a professional couple, both doctors, and their family in 2007 is a neat encapsulation of the social development of Marlow over that period.

The house itself has changed little since it was designed in the style of Sir Christopher Wren. The elegant gazebo built on to the corner of the garden wall fronting West Street has become even more of a landmark as it is gloriously illuminated with a shining silver Christmas tree in December.

Remnantz in West Street is a Grade II listed building and was built in 1720 with three storeys and another wing. The house is named after a Woolwich iron-founder called Stephen Remnant, who inherited it in 1756. From 1802, the junior department of the Royal Military College was based here (as recorded in the plaque shown below) until its move to Sandhurst in 1812-13.

In 1825, Thomas Wethered bought the house from the Remnant family. He moved from the White House in High Street to Remnantz and lived there until his death in 1849. It remained in the Wethered family until 2007. This photograph shows the view in the 1890s looking south from West Street to the front of the mansion, with railings and recently pollarded trees.

Interestingly, Steven and Sally Bosley made exactly the same move, from the White House to Remnantz, in 2007. They first visited the house in 2002 in their business capacity of military auctioneers because they had received the Marlow Drum to be auctioned. This was originally a Russian drum, brought home to Marlow by General Higginson from the Crimea and re-emblazoned by him in the colours of the 1st Buckinghamshire Rifle Volunteers. He added a plaque recording that the drum was presented by him to this newly-formed unit raised at Institute Road, Marlow, in 1859. It was found in a barn in Scotland in 2002 and handed to the Bosleys to auction. Steven Bosley noticed the plaque and realised the local connection; the drum had come home. Anthony Wethered, then living at Remnantz, organised a local subscription and the drum was bought by the town on the occasion of the bicentenary of the RMC. The plaque on the drum reads:

THIS DRUM Taken at Sevastopol Sept. 9th 1855 was presented to the Corps of Drums and
Fifes of Great Marlow. COLONEL HIGGINSON GRENADIER GUARDS 1861.

The land now known as Wethered Park was previously part of the Remnantz Estate and was used as the parade ground by the Royal Military College in the early 1800s.

It is now a gated development of large town houses and apartments, completed in 1998 by developers Charles Church. The refurbished older buildings form an elegant crescent with the new, opening on to communal gardens of around three acres of parkland with private access for the owners of the surrounding houses.

On the face of it, very little appears to have changed at eighteenth-century Grade I-listed Georgian manor house Harleyford Manor since 1960, except perhaps the groundsmen's skills in topiary. Parts of the grounds are attributed to the eighteenth-century landscape designer Capability Brown and have been designated in modern times as an Area of Outstanding Natural Beauty.

In fact, the house and its estate have seen major changes in recent years. The current family owners purchased the estate in 1952 and developed a marina with Thames-side moorings, luxurious holiday homes, residential properties and an eighteen-hole golf course, all in the historic parkland. The holiday homes are only fully available to their owners for eleven months of the year due to planning restrictions.

In 1989, the manor house was converted for office use and a wide range of commercial office space is now available, from 200sq. ft up to 8,000sq. ft. Some office space is based in the marina building while other space is available within some of the historic estate properties. Rents quoted begin from £26 per month plus VAT per sq. ft inclusive.

5

SHOPPING

Eastman's dry cleaning store in High Street was
taken over by Sketchleys, who left Marlow some
time in the 1990s. It is now the Spa-NK cosmetic
and beauty treatment shop; another example
of the change in shopping provision between
everyday and luxury needs.

The light and airy building which is now Brasserie Gérard at 21 High Street, next door to Liston Court, bears little resemblance to the intensively used Freeman Hardy & Willis in the 1920 photograph, or another more recent occupier, the Sun Yah Chinese takeaway restaurant.

The conversion of this listed building in early 1996 rescued it from the English Heritage 'Buildings At Risk' register and extended it backwards to take advantage of its position in Liston Court. The magnificent trees at the back were retained and protected and now provide a backdrop to a pleasant oasis for an al fresco meal as global warming spreads its benefits as well as its threats.

There are now around thirty-two restaurants, sandwich shops and pubs serving food in the immediate centre of Marlow, of which approximately a third are provided by national operators.

In 1976, Mrs Bishop sold this shop at 14-22 West Street and the orchard behind it to Waitrose. Riley Road was built at the same time as the new supermarket. Having sold on the freehold interest, Waitrose took back a twenty-five-year lease of their store which was due to come to an end in December 2009.

Early in 2007, J. Sainsbury plc purchased a head leasehold interest from the freeholders and became Waitrose's landlords. This meant that the usual business renewal of the lease that Waitrose could have expected was no longer available because Sainsbury's wanted to move in.

The supermarket lies within an area known as 'Site M4' in the Local Plan. Sainsbury's has submitted the most recent of several planning applications, although its application covers only the supermarket site rather than the comprehensive development of all of M4. The application was approved early in 2010. Waitrose also had its application to move to Chapel House, 2-8 Liston Road, Marlow, approved. The most recent date given for the move is 16 January 2011. No jobs are expected to be lost in the removal.

Mr W.R. Clark, Family Butcher, finally accepted the inevitable and closed his doors at 22-24 High Street in 1997. Independent food suppliers have become a dying breed all over the country, due to the increasing pressure to provide a quicker, more comprehensive shopping experience, and Marlow has been no exception to this trend.

For national retailers like Monsoon, which took over the larger part of the old Clark butcher's shop, the need to work within the constraints of an historic building appear to be accepted in exchange for a good High Street location in this Thames Valley market town.

Gerrards and Greco have been taken over and converted to a single Clintons Cards store, whose size and predictability is unusual for Marlow High Street.

Mr Barnard (for presumably it is he, standing as he is before Barnard & Sons in Spittal Street), pictured in his long apron in front of 22 Spittal Street in 1910, would be staggered at the range, quality and origins of the food on offer in the shop immediately to the west of his, which is now occupied by Marks & Spencer Simply Food.

Children playing in the street have not been seen in Spittal Street for a very long time. The traffic is particularly heavy through this narrow street, providing the main access into Marlow and through the town to Henley. Dean Street car park has taken over from the houses in the middle of the old picture and all attempts to redevelop this site have so far failed.

The transformation of 22 Spittal Street into a single store, Blooming Marvellous, catering for pregnant mothers and their infants, is one of three such stores in Marlow, probably reflecting two recent social phenomena: the movement out of London of young people just before, or just after, starting a family; and the increased economic buying power of young women, many of whom continue to work throughout the process of having a family.

Alan Coster took over tobacconist's Coster & Son at 52 High Street from his father in 1947, when there were more than twenty retail tobacconists in the area. He finally retired at the age of seventy-six, having built up a considerable commercial trade from his Marlow base and having contributed significantly to the public life of Marlow through the Chamber of Trade (founder Secretary) and the Rotary Club (one-time President).

The small shop units at 50-54 High Street have clung on, providing accommodation for specialist retailers like Fenn Wright Manson, ladies' fashion shop, Crew Clothing Company and JoJo Maman Bébé, providing maternity and babies' wear.

The larger unit previously occupied by estate agent A.C. Frost & Co has been occupied by Pizza Express for more than ten years; this is one example of the increasing numbers of people with the time, money and inclination to spend their leisure hours eating and drinking in Marlow.

Left: Older, less adequate buildings, photographed in 1940, have been redeveloped in recent times. This included the old Picture Palace on the corner (see page 79).

Below: Here is an example of the development that has taken place on both sides of Spittal Street, close to the corner with Dean Street. In this case, we focus on the northern side at 27 Spittal Street. Modern shop units with offices above have replaced the old buildings.

Thanks to its proximity to the City of London, wealthy people have been building large houses in Marlow since the eighteenth century. One of these is Cromwell House at 55 High Street, at the centre of the right-hand side of the early photograph here. Cromwell House was once named Alfred House and was taken by the War Office to accommodate Royal Military College cadets. In 1851, Charles Bloxham, a solicitor, and his family were resident. Edwin Clark was the following occupant.

The property was split into two lots: 41 High Street, which became the offices of Cripps & Shone, and 39 High Street, which was let in 1912 to the Post Office on lease for a term of twenty-one years at £120 per annum until its eventual sale to the Royal Mail. The Post Office moved across the road in 1992 to 44 High Street and Cromwell House remained empty for three years until it became a retail boutique. The ground floor of Cromwell House was initially let to a shoe shop and since January 2004 has been occupied by Insight Opticians, owned by Martin Lloyd. The property is still owned by the Post Office. The trees in front have been replaced by almond trees, covered in fairy lights around Christmas.

The small shop on the corner of High Street and Institute Road has had its bay windows removed and is now Marlow Jeweller's, with a locked door that is only opened on request.

Originally Carters restaurant and then the Atkins Bakery, Burgers was founded in The Causeway in 1942 by Eric and Marie Burger, who came to England from Switzerland in 1936. Their traditional tea room, chocolate shop and bakery have been run in recent years by their two sons, Bernard and Philippe (see page 94).

Although there are persistent rumours of a sale to a national chain, Burgers restaurant continues in family hands. Bernard's father purchased the three cottages alongside and planning permission has recently been obtained to extend a rear single-storey extension behind the first of these. Another CCTV camera can be seen on a pole outside the restaurant.

From the extreme right, Bernard, Eric, Philippe and Susan celebrate Burgers' fiftieth anniversary with staff in 2002. Philippe was in charge of the bakery and looked after the business and manufacturing side of things along with his father, Eric, who has since retired. Bernard looked after the shop and tearoom with his mother, Marie, and he continues to do so.

A photograph of the Burgers' team, taken in 2010. Bernard is still running the shop and tearoom, but with considerably less camouflage.

6

PRINCIPAL BUILDINGS

The Old Vicarage is pictured here in 1840, with the stunning sundial on top of the entry arch. This still survives following the split of The Old Vicarage into flats and the construction of the Rectory behind the arch in 1994-95.

Built in around 1758 for Dr William Battie, the Court Garden Estate was purchased in the 1920s for £9,226 by public subscription initiated by Messrs L.J. Smith, F.H. Carthgate and Canon Graves. In 1926, HRH Princess Mary presented the keys and deeds of the estate to Marlovian General Sir George Higginson, known as 'Father of the Guards', veteran of the Crimean War and (through his friendship with King George V and Queen Mary) godfather to the Princess. He immediately handed these to the Higginson Park Society, which managed the property, and provided a bowling green, a putting green and tennis courts, all of which are still well-used.

A swimming pool, sports hall, café bar, gymnasium and the Shelley Theatre were added and opened on 27 September 1975. Roger Whitehead ARIBA, a partner of Michael Aukett Associates, was the project architect at the time.

The statue of Sir Steve Redgrave on the right of this 2010 photograph was erected in 1996 to commemorate his extraordinary feat of achieving a fourth gold medal for rowing in the Olympic Games. In 2000, he achieved a fifth and took a tour of honour on an open-topped bus around town, culminating in a civic reception in Court Garden House.

It would be hard to think of any circumstances now under which Marlow residents might be roused sufficiently to riot. However, riot they did in 1880 in an attempt to overturn the domination of local landowners, including the Wethereds, in parliamentary elections. The photograph shows the results for the brewery offices in High Street and the White House adjoining.

Since the closure of the Thomas Wethered Brewery in 1988, the left-hand building which used to house their offices, it has been turned into Zizzi's, a pizza restaurant, while the White House next door is now a Jack Wills Ltd clothing store, which caters for well-heeled young people. Jack Wills has refurbished the house more or less as the Wethered family would have occupied it, with a few interesting additions such as knickers displayed in the kitchen fridge.

Albion House, West Street, was the house where the poet Percy Bysshe Shelley (4 August 1792-8 July 1822) and his second wife, Mary Shelley, the authoress, lived in 1817.

In 1816, Thomas Love Peacock, a close friend who already lived in Marlow at 47 West Street, appears to have been entrusted with the task of finding a new home for the Shelleys before they settled at Albion House. Peacock was an English satirist and novelist who repeated the basic setting of his novels – characters at a table discussing and criticising the philosophical opinions of the day. This photograph was taken around 1880, looking east, and shows the frontage of what was Albion House together with the railings of Colonel's Meadow playing field. In 1867, Sir William Robert Clayton, Bart, placed a tablet on the parapet of Albion House inscribed: 'He is gone where all things wise and fair... Death feeds on his mute voice and laughs at our despair.'

Albion House has since been separated into private residences, a row of whitewashed cottages with Gothic windows.

The Great Marlow Institute was founded in 1853 and moved to these premises on Institute Road in 1890. It had a library on the ground floor with newspaper, reading and recreation rooms on the first floor. The county library rented a room here in 1954 and bought the building following the closure of the Institute in 1957. It was reopened as a county library in 1959 and is pictured here in 1980.

The creaky wooden stairs and first-floor reading room were closed to visitors when the large and airy extension was built over the rear garden in 1995. It is now possible to access the internet from one of the four computers here and to use the photocopier, as well as access the usual range of books and large print books, amplified by DVDs and CDs for loan.

Marlow Place was built in 1721, probably by Thomas Archer, for John Wallop, the grandson of Sir William Borlase, the later Earl of Portsmouth. It was used in the early 1800s as an annexe to the junior branch of the Royal Military College at Remnantz.

At first it faced down what was effectively the main road into Marlow, St Peter Street. The original river bridge sprang from the bottom of this street.

Despite being left looking slightly out of place by this development, Marlow Place is still one of two properties in the town today with a Grade I listing – the other being the suspension bridge itself.

In 1949 and 1950 respectively, planning permission was obtained to convert the ground floor into a restaurant and snack bar and then to convert the first floor into a theatre. It was used as a girls' finishing school until 1965 when it was refurbished for office use, and is currently the headquarters of a catering company. In 1971, a planning appeal resulted in a three-storey modern office block being built immediately adjacent.

The Grade I listed building known today as Bisham Abbey, just outside Marlow, is in fact the manor house built around 1260 alongside the now lost monastery which is mentioned in the Domesday Book. In 1310, Queen Elizabeth of the Scots, wife of King Robert the Bruce, her stepdaughter, Princess Marjorie, and sister-in-law, Lady Christine of Carrick, were confined here for two years after their capture on the Isle of Rathlin before being removed to Windsor.

The Abbey fields, now used as a golf course and a training base by the England national football and rugby teams, were used as burial fields during the plague of 1665. Bisham was located as far from London as the funeral carts could come out and still return to London in a single day.

In the late twentieth century, Edward Vansittart's widow gave Bisham Abbey to the nation, covenanted always to be used as a sporting venue for young people in memory of her two sons, killed in the Second World War. It is now one of the UK's National Sports Centres.

Her niece, Margaret Dickinson, was her successor to the title of Lord of the Manor of Bisham and used her unexpected bequest in any number of good ways. The river bank in front of the fence in the picture was rescued using a gift from her. This generosity is recorded on a board planted at the site.

In 1624, Sir William Borlase founded the grammar school in its present location on West Street, for twenty-four boys to be educated and trained in memory of his son Henry, MP for Marlow, who died in that year.

Some 250 years later, and after a major building programme, the school was reopened as a boys' grammar school in 1881. This photograph, taken in 1890, shows some of the boys standing in the street outside, something current pupils would not risk today.

Above left: Funding for girls' education was less available and it took 364 years before Borlase and the benefits of its consistent funding were made available to girls in 1988. The fight to turn co-educational had taken over eight years. Since then, there have been many improvements and this 2010 photograph shows the relatively new classrooms added at the western end of the old buildings.

Above right: Set into the brick and flint of the original building is the plaque to the memory of Basil Horsfall VC, a student at Borlase between 1903 and 1905. He was a Second Lieutenant, 3rd Battalion East Lancashire Regiment, attached to 11th Battalion. Born on 4 October 1887 in Ceylon (now Sri Lanka), he was killed in action on 27 March 1918, aged thirty. The Digest of his Citation reads:

> On 27 March 1918, between Moyenville and Ablainzeville, France, when the enemy first attacked Second Lieutenant Horsfall's centre platoon, his three forward sections were driven back and he was wounded in the head. Nevertheless, he immediately reorganised the remainder of his men and made a counter-attack which recovered his original position. Despite the severity of his wound, he refused to go to the dressing station as the three remaining officers in his company were casualties. Later, he made a second successful counter-attack but when finally ordered to withdraw, he was the last to leave the position. He was killed almost immediately afterwards.

For this extraordinary valour in the final German offensive of 1918, he was posthumously awarded the Victoria Cross.

The Compleat Angler building is 400 years old and has some connection with Izaak Walton's *The Compleat Angler*, although not so direct a connection as one may think. This scene of the compact buildings was taken looking south-east from the bridge some time in the 1930s. The Compleat Angler started its life as a very small inn owned by Wethereds Brewery and was known as the Riverside Inn, boasting six rooms. In 1888 the landlord of the Compleat Angler was Mr Robert Kilby, who subsequently bought the hostelry from the brewery in 1923. It was later sold to Forte Hotels and is currently owned by Macdonald Hotels.

Some hotel bedrooms are in buildings converted from other uses, whilst some are in twentieth-century extensions to the various main parts of the building. The buildings themselves follow the arc of the river, and are fronted by the river and an enormous weir – begging to be put to use for generating hydro power in these days of the greening of our society.

One can still see in the internal design and layout the unmistakable signs of Olga Polizzi's touch, who, as one of the Forte family, headed their design division and was responsible for upgrading the Heritage division.

The restaurants provide guests with the opportunity to eat and drink with the backdrop of the river and its wildlife; the hotel also owns fishing rights along the bank. The hotel helps to support the cost of the external lighting of the opposite bank and its beautiful Victorian church.

Above: The Town Clock on the tower above the Crown was given to the town in 1805 by Pascoe Grenfell, the MP for Great Marlow between 1807 and 1819, an associate of Sir Thomas Williams, the copper baron. Williams presented the market building to Marlow in 1807 as a Town Hall, comprised of a covered market, fire station and assembly room. The sequence of these dates suggests that the clock might originally have been placed on the seventeenth-century market house, which stood in the middle of Market Square.

Left: In collaboration with Marlow Town Council, the 'Tempus Fugit' group, led by Tony Shannon, was set up to restore the Town Clock in time for its bicentenary on 3 April 2005.

The work included restoration of the face and turret and removal of the original works, replacing them with a modern electric drive and striking system. On Tuesday 11 March 2008 at 7 p.m., Marlow Town Council met and agreed an expenditure of £410 to install an independent electrical supply to the Town Clock.

7

PUBLIC SERVICES

Marlow Fire Brigade is no longer guardian to the old fire machine. In 2009, the men are mean machines themselves, highly trained and regularly drilled. Their protection now extends to French-style helmets, with built-in drop-down visors and the very latest in heatproof gear.

This fine and proud body of firemen, gathered around their fire engine, might have appreciated the irony that their fire station in the building known as the Crown now houses a kitchen shop. Kitchen fires still account for a proportion of their successors' workload, balanced by their indefatigable work to inform the public of the dangers of kitchen fires through public displays.

From a purpose-built fire station at the junction of Cambridge Road and Dean Street, the service moved again in August 2005 to a strategic location just off the Marlow bypass, allowing them to cover a wider area. The majority of 'shouts' these days relate to road traffic accidents.

Above left: The original premises for the doctors' practice which eventually combined with other doctors to form The Doctors' House was located at The Old Stone House on West Street. One of the principal consulting rooms was the main room at the rear, with exquisite Dutch tiles which still survive. The building is now home to a firm of solicitors.

Above right: The modern doctors' surgery is still known as The Doctors' House, but is now a new building off Victoria Road alongside the Marlow Community Hospital. The Marlow Medical Group has its own website at http://www.marlowdoctors.co.uk, where a patient can make an appointment or request a prescription online and find out about the other services the doctors and their associates provide. The practice is a training practice and has been for a considerable time.

Above left: Marlow Post Office was located in Cromwell House in the middle of High Street for many years. In the early 1990s it was moved across the road into 44 High Street, but eventually closed in 2008.

Above right: From the gracious surroundings of the original seventeenth-century building, it had slipped to a temporary building in the Dean Street car park, labelled a 'third world shack' by Canadian visitors recently. It has recently moved to a permanent building on Institute Road.

The small court and police station building on Trinity Road must have been quite cramped.

The current police station on Dean Street offers a 'Tier 2' service, which is a neighbourhood station covered by station duty officers (SDOs). As well as all Tier 1 services, the SDOs offer the following: road traffic collision reporting; crime recording (either in person or via telephone to the Police Enquiry Centre); processing of documents after a vehicle seizure; changing of details for immigration and nationality purposes; receipt of property connected with a crime; bail signing; helping stranded people; dealing with complaints; and providing guidance on subject access request procedures.

8

CHURCHES AND PLACES OF WORSHIP

A copy of an engraving showing All Saints' Church under reconstruction, as viewed looking north-west from the Thames just downstream of the bridge in 1832. Work started that year on the new church. The parish church of Marlow is a spacious Gothic structure and has a wooden spire, erected in 1627 between the nave and chancel. The most remarkable monuments are those of Sir Miles Hobart, one of the Members of Parliament for this borough who was killed when his coach overturned as it was going down Holborn Hill in 1632; and Katherine, wife of Sir William Willoughby, who was Sheriff of the County in 1603.

Formerly known as Christ Church, the Independent United Reformed Church once housed a Sunday school and used to be a Dissenting meeting house. The history of Dissenters goes back over 300 years in Marlow. In 1662, an attempt by Charles II to impose his will on the Church of England led to 2,000 clergymen leaving their parishes in dissent. There is a record of a visiting preacher called Samuel Pomfret, who came to the town in 1693, but he was probably not the first to preach against the Act of Uniformity.

The United Reformed Church was formed in 1972 by the union of the Congregational Church in England and Wales and the Presbyterian Church of England. It continues to express its deep commitment to the visible unity of the whole Church. In 1981 it entered into union with the Reformed Churches of Christ, and in the year 2000 with the Congregational Union of Scotland. Christ Church Sunday school was provided for local children attending local schools. Now very much a family church where children are welcome to the Junior Church, Kool Kids and Icthus meetings take place at the same time as the main services. This photograph, taken in 2009, shows the extension added to the old building.

Left: Looking east, a view of St Peter's Roman Catholic Church in 1980 from the graveyard. This church was designed by Pugin in 1846. A school was built and added close by within the same grounds. In 1969 an extension was added as the congregation outgrew the size of the church. The church contains a relic said to be the hand of St James. Eventually a new school was built in Prospect Road and all its pupils moved to the new location in 1978. The old Pugin rooms remain and the old school building has been rebuilt and is now used for church events and recreational use.

Below: The church's congregation in 2009 is currently 400, which has dropped 40 per cent since the late 1970s. An ecclesiastical census was carried out throughout England on 30 March 1851 to record the attendance at all places of worship. The Records for Great Marlow's St Peter's Church was recorded as ninety-three morning congregation and scholars and sixty-eight evening congregation and scholars. The drop in congregations is nationwide, not just peculiar to Marlow.

Above: Outside St Peter's Roman Catholic Church in the summer of 1973, Felicity (left) beside twin-sister Cecelia (co-author), stand on the steps of the old part of the church following their first Holy Communion ceremony. A person's first reception of the sacrament of the Eucharist is celebrated by Roman Catholics, who believe this event to be very important and a central focus of the church.

Left: Daisy, standing beside her mother, Felicity, and Aunt Cecelia, who are coincidentally standing in the same place and position as their younger selves, at a relative's Holy Communion ceremony in 2000.

St Peter's School pupils opposite the Pugin Rooms in 1973 at their Holy Communion ceremony. Louisa and Felicity (left) and Cecelia and Teresa (right).

In the year of the millennium, Jake, a pupil of St Peter's School, happily celebrates his Holy Communion. He is in the centre of the photograph between his brothers Elliot and Felix.

Looking north-west, a view of Holy Trinity Church and graveyard in 1991. The church was built in 1852 and closed in 1975. After its closure, the church was converted into offices without disturbing the graveyard.

Holy Trinity Church of England School, opposite the church in Wethered Road, was built in 1961 and is still open today with 287 children attending. The children still sing in the choir, which has moved to All Saints' Church by the river.

Looking across the Thames from Anglers Lawn at the Compleat Angler hotel, a view of Marlow Bridge and church, *c.* 1910. Dedicated to All Saints', the parish church dates back to the twelfth century, with records showing that a church existed in 1070 when St Wulfstarn, Bishop of Worcester, visited the town. Over the years the foundations had decayed due to flooding and the old church was demolished to make way for the new one. The chancel was later added in 1867. The spire and tower were altered again in 1898-99.

This photograph was taken in 2010 from the Compleat Angler hotel's lawn and shows a remarkably similar view of the church and bridge.

Looking north, a view of the old Methodist Chapel in Spittal Street in 1900. There was a Wesleyan chapel (named after John Wesley, who founded Methodism in 1738) on the same site in 1810 which was later replaced by the larger building in the photo. In 1885 the Anchor Brewery and yard, which was on the same site, was purchased by a group of local businessmen and trustees of the church and then sold on to the church. The church contained 200 seats or 'sittings' of which seventy were 'free', i.e. they were not subject to pew rents. Between 1841 to 1934 there was another church in Marlow called the Primitive Methodist Church. The 'Prims', as they were known, were a breakaway denomination of the Wesleyans. Their first church was in Cambridge Road and in 1875 they moved to a larger building which is now Liston Hall. The principal strands of Methodism united locally in Marlow in 1934 when the Primitive Methodist Church closed.

In 1989 the present hall on the right-hand side of the Methodist church was added. A front foyer extension, officially called the 'Welcome Area', was built in 2000.

9

LEISURE, FESTIVALS AND ANNUAL EVENTS

In 1928, a large group of children is assembled outside the Picture Palace cinema on the corner of Dean Street and Spittal Street. In 2010, there is no cinema in Marlow. The larger towns like High Wycombe, with two, and Maidenhead have cinemas now. Each has several screens to show multiple films at the same time.

Marlow Fair in 1897 looks to have taken up High Street in the same way as nearby towns such as Abingdon and High Wycombe close their streets for similar events.

In modern times, the Marlow Fair has appeared over the weekend of Marlow Regatta in Court Gardens Park for years. When the Marlow Regatta moved to Dorney Lake and the local regatta changed to the Town Regatta, the fair remained unchanged. The park is transformed into a magical place of lights, music and high activity as teenagers challenge one another to the latest stomach-churning addition to the Traylens' stable. One sad loss last year was the remarkably accurate fortune teller, but the dodgems, carousel and candy floss showed that tradition flourishes at least in this part of Marlow. For more information, people can access the fair's website at: http://www.traylensfunfair.co.uk.

Children playing on swings and a climbing frame in Marlow in October 1964 would no doubt be impressed by the new playground installed in Higgingson Park in 2007. It includes exciting and varied play equipment. Always busy on Saturdays and Sundays, a new purpose-built café alongside the park area means that parents and friends can sit and be comfortable at the same time as keeping an eye on their children.

The Coronation of Queen Elizabeth II in 1953 generated a sustained and creative response in Marlow. For weeks beforehand, a cross-section of the community laboured to produce street decorations (from solid wood, without a jig-saw in sight) and carnival floats.

For some reason, the tradition of building floats and staging carnivals fell into disuse around the mid-1990s in Marlow, as in most other towns in the UK, although some do of course still survive. The celebrations of the Golden Jubilee of Queen Elizabeth II in 2002 were intended by her to be both a commemoration of her fifty years as monarch and an opportunity for her officially and personally to thank her people for their loyalty.

The celebrations took the form of demonstrations of dancing and singing by schoolchildren in Bisham when she arrived by boat at Bisham Abbey.

In the face of global warming threats, the last winter (2009/10) has been exceptionally cold and the Thames has frozen in restricted areas for short periods. However, this has been nothing like 1890 when Marlow residents had the good fortune to be able to skate on the river.

Most people have far more leisure time in the early twenty-first century and use the river at Marlow extensively for light relief, such as the annual raft race which used to be held in September each year; the event shown here took place in 1986. Local clubs arrange canoeing and kayaking, there's rowing in the little boats available to hire off Higginson Park and sailing from Marlow Sailing Club at Temple. Many people practise hard for regattas or Olympics from Marlow Rowing Club at the bridge.

Pupils from Marlow Riding School in 1937 doing a musical ride and games on horseback during a gymkhana event. The land is now Globe Business Park. Marlow Riding School was started by Margaret Pinches in 1932 with two of her own leisure horses and became a fully fledged riding school following popular demand. Eventually it was to employ five grooms with forty horses and many volunteers. After the war, ponies were bought so that local children could ride. Vivienne Lee and James Mason were known to have visited for riding, as well as Prince Leka Zog, the Albanian king's son, who lived nearby and rode with an armed bodyguard following him by foot.

Children from Red Barn Riding School are seen here practising their modern gymkhana skills in 2010. Many people around Marlow own and ride horses, and there are regular shows in which they can compete and improve their skills.

Armistice Day in 1960 shows local people actively taking part in the service standing in front of the George and Dragon. An outdoor service, whatever the weather, was preceded by a procession down High Street. Then as now, it provides a vivid witness to the strength of feeling behind the service of Remembrance.

In the same place in 2005, young men representing all parts of the defence forces stand respectfully around the Cenotaph on The Causeway. In 2010, we have been at war in Afghanistan for seven years.

Left: The Chequers Hotel has been a fixture on the High Street in Marlow since before this early photograph was taken in 1940.

Below: The later photograph shows the same buildings in 2005, now with the emphasis on the downstairs bars, appealing to the young with karaoke nights and dancing.

In early 2010, the building stands empty and boarded up, awaiting the resolution of a structural fault in the building. This has since been rectified and the pub will be reopening in the summer.

A comparison of the 1935 photos with the modern photos of public houses; the Ship on West Street and the Coach and Horses on the corner of West Street and High Street suggest something enduring about the publican trade. Both these public houses have adapted to the current emphasis on food with a drink to respect the requirement not to drink and drive. The Coach and Horses specialises in Chinese food.

In the 1980s the Regal cinema in Station Road was showing *Man at the Top*, next door to Marlow Place, where King George IV is supposed to have stayed. The last film to be shown there was *Return of the Jedi* before the cinema was demolished in the mid-1980s.

On the same site in 2010, a modern office building provides offices for a business which 'partners with organisations to bring demonstrable improvements to their project and business performance through the provision of Portfolio, Programme and Project Management consultancy, the delivery of tailored training, the supply of talented resources and the implementation of the appropriate, class-leading Microsoft EPM and SharePoint technologies.' Perhaps we could do with those Jedi back...

10

PEOPLE

'There were sweet dreams in the night/Of time long past
And was it sadness or delight/Each day a shadow onward cast
Which made us wish it yet might last/That time long past.'

Percy Bysshe Shelley's excerpt, taken from his poem 'Time Long Past', was composed in 1819. The poet and his wife lived in Albion House in West Street in 1817, where Shelley produced a number of famous poems. At this time, he also wrote revolutionary political tracts signed 'The Hermit of Marlow'. Queen Mab, as shown in the photograph, was his first major lengthy narrative philosophical poem, dedicated to his first wife, Harriet. Summer days at Marlow were spent on the river and picnicking at Cliveden and Bisham Woods. Shelley was well known in Marlow, talking with poor families, handing out money and giving simple medical advice. He was known to have purchased thick ex-Army blankets and sheets as Christmas presents for the poor of the district. They were embroidered with his name 'pbs Esq' so that they could not be sold off. Albion House was to be the last home in England where the English Romantic poet and his wife Mary, their children and household lived together before leaving for Italy.

Above left: Mary Shelley completed her famous book, *Frankenstein*, in Marlow. The picture shows a copy of the book illustration from an early edition. It is known to have been the first science fiction book ever produced. At the time, sensational reviews were coming in from the journals and distinguished writers were signifying their approval of the then unknown author. During her stay in Marlow, Mary wrote that, 'Marlow was inhabited by a very poor population. The women are lace-makers and lose their health by sedentary labour, for which they are very ill paid. The Poor-laws ground to the dust not only the paupers, but those who had risen just above that state, and were obliged to pay poor-rates.' (Horsham Museum)

Above right: A portrait of Leigh Hunt, who was great friends with the Shelleys and often visited their household with his family. Leigh Hunt was a poet and editor of the *Examiner* and other quarterly magazines. He was instrumental in defending Shelley's poetry, particularly in his articles.

The former Crown & Anchor pub was the venue for the Marlow Poetry Society, which had their inaugural meeting on the premises in 2000. The society, the first of its kind in Marlow, was founded by Cecelia Anne Sadek for a small group of writers and poets (notably including some famous poets and authors). Poetry readings are held in various locations around the town, as well as by the Thames and at outdoor events. The earliest mention of the Crown & Anchor, known to have been frequented by the poet Percy Bysshe Shelley, is in the County Records dated 1757. The pub is no longer in operation and the premises is leased out to businesses.

Jerome K. Jerome photographed in Monks Corner, his home in Marlow Common, beneath the portrait of him by De Laszlo. Jerome was a prolific writer whose work has been translated into many foreign languages but, as Jerome himself said, 'It is as the author of *Three Men in a Boat* that the public persists in remembering me.' It was only in the mid-1870s that the Thames had been discovered as a pleasure-ground. Boating on the Thames became the latest craze: in 1888, the year in which Jerome wrote *Three Men in a Boat*, there were 8,000 registered boats on the river; by the following year there were 12,000. Jerome was therefore writing about the 'in thing' – the book doubtless swelled the numbers who took to boating. 'At first,' recalled Jerome, 'we would have the river almost to ourselves... and sometimes would fix up a trip of three or four days or a week, doing the thing in style and camping out.' (Jerome K Jerome Society)

Monks Corner, a large detached five-bedroom house in Marlow Common, was the home of Jerome K. Jerome in 1910. The outside of this house and adjoining quarters to the left have several panels of both coloured and terracotta designs by Conrad Dressler, erected when Dressler was living in what was then called The White Cottage. During Jerome's stay he was known to utilise a beautiful mosaic table in the property to help inspire the writing of his plays by using small toy figures as characters moving around an imagined stage upon its surface.

Tony Buzan, the famous inventor of the revolutionary Mind Maps, has achieved the status of 'guru', an accolade accorded to very few. He has worked with businesses all over the world to teach them how to maximise the use of their brains. A prolific author, he has written more than ninety books, translated into thirty-three languages and with sales in over 150 countries. The Mind Map is now used by a staggering 250 million people worldwide. Tony moved to Harleyford, Marlow, in 1982, where he made his home and set up his offices at the Harleyford Manor Estate. Along with his Buzan World Enterprises, Tony trained Olympic rowers for the 1988 Seoul, 1992 Barcelona and 2000 Sydney Olympics. One of the main driving forces of Tony's life is poetry; the reading of it, the memorisation of it and the writing of it. Tony's support for the Marlow Poetry Society, along with his delivery of highly interesting poetry, gave the group much food for thought. He is a prolific poet, with over 4,000 poems to his name in subjects ranging from nature and love to describing the universe. He presents his 'poem of the week' on his Buzan World website.

Thomas Williams (1737-1802) was a prominent attorney and active in the copper industry. About 1785, Williams became chief agent of copper mines owned partly by the Earl of Uxbridge and partly by the family of Llysdulas; for a time both parties entrusted the management to Williams alone. He was closely associated with the Uxbridge family and helped several sons get elected to Parliament. In 1790, probably with help from the Earl of Uxbridge, he was elected for Great Marlow and held the seat until his death on 30 November 1802. The seat was won in 1820 by his grandson and retained until 1868.

Paul Goodman, MP for High Wycombe and Marlow up until the election in May 2010, was first elected to Parliament in June 2001. He served on the Select Committee on Work and Pensions and the Select Committee on Deregulation and Regulatory Reform, and as Parliamentary Private Secretary to Rt Hon. David Davis MP until 2003. His top local campaigning priority since then has been the future of Wycombe Hospital. Paul helped to form the all-party Save Hospital Services Committee during the last Parliament, which campaigned against these cuts. In 2005 he was named Health Parliamentarian of the Year by the Patients Association. After the 2005 General Election, Paul was made Shadow Minister for Childcare and Shadow Economic Secretary. In 2007, he was made Shadow Minister for Communities and Local Government. He has co-authored 'Healthy Choice for the Future', a pamphlet about health services. He has taken a special interest in issues connected with flooding in Marlow.

June Coleridge in her garden at Fisherman's Retreat, overlooked by St Peter's Church, taken in September 2009. The Coleridge family tree starts with Mr Nicholas Coleridge, born in 1678. The famous poet and philosopher Samuel Taylor Coleridge, born in 1772, was the ancestor of Antony Duke Coleridge, born in 1915. Antony and June met in Cornwall and wed in 1952. Antony was a solicitor before the war and they moved to Marlow in 1954 for the purpose of joining Cripps & Shone Solicitors, based in West Street, Marlow. The couple set up home at Chanters, opposite Borlase School in West Street. June moved to her current home at Fisherman's Retreat in 2000.

Baron Geoffrey Duke Coleridge (1877-1955) was Justice of the Peace for Devon between 1929 and 1952. The photograph of him here has been taken from a framed painting in June Coleridge's sitting room at Fisherman's Retreat in Marlow. Antony Duke Coleridge, late husband of June, was a direct descendant of the Baron.

June's life since living in Marlow has been very much involved with the local Red Cross. She was Director of Bucks Red Cross for ten years, a voluntary position covering all of Buckinghamshire. June's daughter, Gill, is a well-known literary agent and her youngest son, David, played cricket for Marlow Cricket Club. This photograph was taken in recent years at the Red Cross Centre with Opportunity playgroup, which was started in Marlow by June to help raise funds for the centre. It has since become an independent playgroup.

Eric and Marie Burger shown on their fiftieth wedding anniversary outside Burgers in 1986. Established in 1942, Burgers was formed after a partnership with Marie's uncle in a similar business in Cheltenham eventually led Eric and Marie to start their own successful business elsewhere. They chose Marlow and Burgers success over sixty-eight years has grown ever since. Famous for their handmade Swiss-style chocolates adapted to suit the English taste, as well as their beautifully made celebration cakes, Burgers is still a family-run artisan business. There are fewer privately owned bakeries and tea shops existing in England today, just as the tradition of the family-run business has declined to the extent of surviving one generation only.

Heston Blumenthal, described as a culinary alchemist, spent his childhood years local to Marlow, where he still lives with his wife and three children. At the age of fifteen Heston was exposed to the wonderful world of gastronomy in France and was immediately consumed by it. His attributes, which soon became the trademarks of his success, came from learning the rudiments of French cuisine from books and his trips to France to visit restaurants, vineyards, cheese makers, butchers and artisan producers. In August 1995, this self-taught chef opened The Fat Duck restaurant, which gained three Michelin stars in 2004. A year later it was proclaimed the 'Best Restaurant in the World' by the '50 Best' Academy of over 600 international food critics, journalists and chefs. In 2006 he was awarded an OBE for his contribution to British gastronomy. In 2008 and 2009 he was accredited with the highest score by the *Good Food Guide*, a 10/10, and nominated the 'Best Restaurant in the UK'. His work on television has seen him nominated for a Bafta for *Heston Blumenthal – In Search of Perfection*, and his work with Channel 4 has produced two series of *Feast*, where he creates one-off dining experiences inspired by a period in history. He also starred in *Big Chef Takes on Little Chef*, which saw him revamp the iconic British motorway services chain Little Chef.

Edwin Clark, an eminent Victorian engineer, was born in Marlow in 1814. From his retirement in 1879 to his death in 1894, he lived at Cromwell House on the High Street. Clark was consulting engineer to the Great Marlow Railway which opened in 1873. He is chiefly remembered as the designer of the Anderton Boat Lift, built in 1875 near Cheshire, which links the navigable stretch of the River Weaver with the Trent and Mersey Canal. In 1846 he met Robert Stephenson, who appointed him superintending engineer of the Menai Suspension Bridge in Wales which opened in 1850. Later that year he became an engineer with the Electric & International Telegraph Co., where he took out the first of several patents for telegraph apparatus. The London and North Western Railway used Clark's telegraph between London and Rugby. This photograph shows a portrait of Edwin Clark, *c.* 1880. A plaque on Cromwell House was unveiled in October 1994 by the President of the Institute of Civil Engineers to commemorate this great engineer.

Sir Steve Redgrave, five-time Olympic gold medallist rower, grew up in Marlow Bottom and attended Great Marlow School. He has proved himself the greatest Olympian Britain has ever produced. After striking gold in Sydney 2000, he became our only athlete ever to have won gold medals at five consecutive Olympic Games in an endurance sport. Now off the water, Steve is absorbed in motivational speaking and commercial and charitable projects. The Steve Redgrave Trust forged its way beyond the £5 million target that Steve set when launching the charity in 2001. Steve has now teamed up with Sport Relief and joined the Comic Relief family to form the Steve Redgrave Fund. Higginson Park features a bronze statue of Sir Steve looking across the river towards the location of the finishing line of the Marlow Town Regatta. There is also a road, Redgrave Place, in Marlow named to commemorate the Olympic medallist.

Other titles published by The History Press

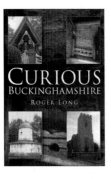

Curious Buckinghamshire
ROGER LONG

Curious Buckinghamshire is a guide to over 100 unusual and extraordinary sights from all parts of the county. Illustrated with a range of photographs and original drawings, Roger Long's entertaining stories will inspire Buckinghamshire residents and visitors alike to greater exploration of both familiar and unknown sights of this historically rich and curious county.

978 0 7524 5516 7

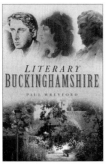

Literary Buckinghamshire
PAUL WREYFORD

Poet John Betjemen was not the only scribe 'beckoned out to lanes in beechy Bucks'. Many of the country's most famous writers shared his fondness for the county and sought solace within its boundaries. John Milton came here to escape the plague in London; Enid Blyton fled the capital's increasing development, while D.H. Lawrence and his German wife took refuge on the outbreak of the First World War.

978 0 7509 4959 0

Villages Around Maidenhead
LUKE OVER

Over the past twenty-five years Luke Over has written 300 articles chronicling the history of Maidenhead and its surrounding villages. These range from pre-historic landscapes through the Roman, Saxon and Medieval periods to the present day. This volume is based on a selection of these articles covering the origins of East Berks and South Bucks villages, offering a wealth of information to anyone interested in the history of this popular Berkshire area.

978 0 7524 5289 0

The Changing Thames
BRIAN EADE

In his long-awaited new book, Brian Eade returns to his beloved Thames for a third time. In a collection of over 200 photographs he compares scenes from days gone by with contemporary views, all the way from the river's source in Gloucestershire to Teddington Lock. This affectionate portrait of the Thames illustrates the changing face Britain's favourite river and will delight river people and visitors alike.

978 0 7509 4779 4

Visit our website and discover thousands of other History Press books.
www.thehistorypress.co.uk